Thomas Richardson and Sons

Veronica, or, The Holy Face of Our Lord Jesus Christ

An Historical Notice of this Signal and Most Holy Major Relic of the Basilica

of the Vatican of St. Peter

Thomas Richardson and Sons

Veronica, or, The Holy Face of Our Lord Jesus Christ
An Historical Notice of this Signal and Most Holy Major Relic of the Basilica of the Vatican of St. Peter

ISBN/EAN: 9783337258771

Printed in Europe, USA, Canada, Australia, Japan

Cover: Foto ©Lupo / pixelio.de

More available books at **www.hansebooks.com**

THE TRUE LIKENESS
of the
HOLY FACE OF OUR LORD J. C.
Which is preserved and Venerated at
Rome in the Vatican Basilica
of St. Peter.

Multi dicunt: Quis ostendit nobis Bona ? Signatum est super nos lumen Vultus tui Domine.—Ps. iv. 7.

"Many say, Who showeth us good things ? The light of Thy countenance, O Lord, is signed upon us."

VERONICA;

OR,

THE HOLY FACE

OF

OUR LORD JESUS CHRIST.

AN

HISTORICAL NOTICE

OF THIS MOST HOLY RELIC OF THE

VATICAN BASILICA OF ST. PETER,

WITH PRAYERS, INDULGENCES, ETC.

TRANSLATED FROM THE FRENCH.

"Respice in faciem Christi tui."—*Ps.* 83.

LONDON:
THOMAS RICHARDSON AND SON,
DUBLIN; AND DERBY.
NEW YORK: HENRY H. RICHARDSON AND CO.
MDCCCLXX.

*A solis ortu usque ad occasum, laudabile
nomen Domini.*—Ps. cxii. 3.

From the rising of the Sun to the going down of the
same, the name of the Lord is worthy of praise.

HISTORICAL NOTICE[*]

OF

THE VERONICA, OR HOLY FACE.

The Holy Face, or Veronica, is one of the three great, remarkable and very holy relics which the patriarchal Basilica of St. Peter of the Vatican preserves with a jealous care, and which have been in every age of the Church, the object of the veneration of the faithful. The Veronica, is a veil, or handkerchief, on which is impressed the true likeness of the adorable face of our Lord and Saviour Jesus Christ, miraculously imprinted, not produced by artificial colours, but by the divine power of God the Son made Man.

These precious relics are preserved in an

[*] The greater number of documents which compose this Notice, are taken from the articles, "Volto Santo" et 'Veronica" "du Dizionario di erudizione Storico-ecclesiastica di Cavaliere Gaetano Moroni, 2. Ajutante di Camera di SS. Pio IX.," published at Venice, 1861.

oratory situated in the interior of one of the four large pentagonal pillars, which support the magnificent cupola, at the epistle side of the papal altar. Paul V. placed the Holy Face there in 1606, and Urban VIII., the holy Lance in 1625, and the wood of the true Cross in 1629.

From a constant tradition, which is founded on the most authentic documents, we are informed, that whilst our Saviour was on the painful journey to Calvary, loaded with the heavy wood of the cross, the altar on which He was to sacrifice His life for the redemption of mankind, a holy woman, moved by compassion, presented Him a handkerchief, or towel, to wipe His face, all covered with sweat, spittle, dust, and blood; and that Jesus, having used it, gave it back to her, having impressed on it His majestic and venerable image, so full of the deep sorrow into which He was then plunged by the weight of the sins of the world.

It is for this reason, that this holy woman is usually represented near our Saviour, holding in her hands the Holy Face, as may be seen in the sixth station of the holy way of the cross.

The learned Piazza, in his work entitled,

"Emerologio di Roma," which was published in 1713, relates this pious tradition on the feast of St. Veronica, the 4th of February. St. Veronica, a noble lady of Jerusalem, lived about the year 38 of the Christian era, during the reign of the Emperor Tiberius. It is believed that she is the woman that was cured of the bloody flux by our Lord, and whom Baronius calls Berenicia, being called Veronica, from the circumstance of her having possessed the blessed relic of the Holy Face. After Jesus had left the house of Pilate, and was on His way to Calvary to be put to death, being all covered with blood from the scourges which He had received, and the wounds of His blessed temples, which were caused by the crown of sharp thorns; after having gone 450 steps, He came near to a house which formed an angle, where, Veronica seeing Him approach in the distance, through compassion, went to meet Him, and, taking the veil from off her head, presented it to Him to wipe His face, all covered with sweat and blood. Our Lord benignly received it from her hands, having wiped His face with it, returned it to her with the impress of His Holy Face printed

on it.* A gracious acknowledgment, but
with a resemblance so natural, that the
marks of the fingers of the cruel man
who had given Him the sacrilegious blow,
are quite visible. Veronica, full of joy at
possessing so precious a treasure, piously
cared it till the arrival at Jerusalem, from
Rome, of the ambassadors whom Tiberius
on being informed by Pilate of the great
number of miracles which Jesus had performed, had sent in the hope that he likewise might be cured of a malady with which
he was afflicted. When the envoys of the
Emperor arrived, they found that Jesus had
been crucified, and heard from the Jews the
fable of His disciples stealing His body, and
pretending that it had arisen, but Veronica
undeceived them by showing them the towel
with the Holy Face of our Lord impressed
upon it. She promised to accompany them
to Rome, and likewise told them that at the
sight of the holy relic the Emperor would be
cured. Having placed the Holy Face in a
case, or shrine, she set out with the ambassadors for Rome, where, having presented it
to the Emperor, he was instantly cured.

* Brev. Ambr. Petr. in Catal.

This is why Tiberius wished to honour Jesus Christ by placing a statue to Him in the Lararium, or chapel, where the Romans kept their household gods; but the Roman Senate would not allow it, "on the principle," says Baronius, "that they would not give that worship to a mortal which was due to a god."*

Cardinal Baronius, in his "Ecclesiastical Annals"† of the year of our Lord, 34, after he had spoken of the shroud which enveloped the head of our Saviour in the sepulchre, said, "Now, this shroud is different from that which Berenicia gave our Blessed Redeemer to wipe His Face all covered with sweat and blood, and on which remained the impress of His adorable Face, according to the tradition of the Christians, and testimony of an ancient manuscript‡ which is preserved

* It appears that the senate was angry because Pilate sent the account of the Passion and Resurrection of Christ to the Emperor Tiberius, and not to them, as was customary. It is likewise certain that the governors of provinces wrote directly to the emperor on great and urgent occasions.

† Translated by Pierre Coppin, D.D., Curé of Notre Dame du Valles, Paris.

‡ Alveri, in his "Roma in ogni Stato," vol. ii., page 210, gives us the history of Veronica, taken from an ancient manuscript of Nicholas Signorile, inscribed in the Vatican library, No. 3351.

in the Vatican library, and that mentions it
was brought to Rome." Bishop Methodius,
an ancient chronographer, speaks of this
Berenicia, likewise called Veronica, and of
the image of our Saviour impressed on the
veil.

Very many writers testify the truth of this
fact, authenticated by a perpetual and unin-
terrupted tradition; we will quote some in
the course of this notice. We will content
ourselves to cite in this place what the
learned Bishop of Sarnelli affirms in his
" *Letters on ecclesiastical subjects ;*" that all
the writers on the Holy Land, and especially
Adricomio, say that the house of Veronica
was situated on the same route on which
Jesus went to Calvary, and that everything
occurred that we have already related.

Although the act attributed to Veronica
may appear to us somewhat extraordinary,
we are, however, less astonished when we
know that a custom prevailed among the
Jewish women of wearing on the head or
neck a veil of linen or cotton, which they
presented to persons as a mark of friendship,
when they saw their face covered with sweat
or bathed in tears. Such is, in effect, the
primary meaning of the word *suaire*, which

Bergièr thus defines in his theological dictionary: "A handkerchief or linen, used to wipe the face." Veronica not only conformed to the received custom of her nation, but she had to brave the fury of the cruel soldiers, and also the wicked treatment of the violent and bloodthirsty populace. But she merited by her devotion to Him, in having His sacred image impressed on her handkerchief, as a mark of eternal love; this is why the heroic action of this woman will be glorified in every age, and pious souls will not cease to bless her for this service and this honour rendered to Jesus in His dolorous agony.

Valerius Maximus speaks of another Berenicia, which Pliny calls Pherenicia, who, by an exceptional favour, was allowed to be present at the Olympic games, which was not allowed to other women. But far greater and still more exalted was the glory given to our Berenicia, by the image of the Holy Face being impressed on her handkerchief by our Saviour. The prize obtained by the conquerors at the Olympic games, was a laurel crown; for Berenicia, the highest glory was a head crowned with thorns; it is for this reason, that the hymn composed in honour of Holy Face, by Pope John XXII., who was created Sovereign Pontiff at Avignon in 1316, says—

"Salve, sancta Facies nostri Redemptoris,
In qua nitet species divini decoris
Impressa panniculo nivei candoris
Dataque Veronicæ signum ob amoris."

Hail! O Blessed Face of our Redeemer,
Face pure, where shines celestial splendour
Upon linen white divinely impress'd,
A pledge of love to Veronica blest.

As we have seen in the touching relation of Piazza, it is generally believed, that St. Veronica is no other than the woman cured of the bloody flux by our Saviour. In an historical manuscript in the Grecian language, translated into Latin by P. Combefis, and printed at Paris in 1664, we read: "That the woman's name was Berenicia, who was cured by our Saviour of the bloody flux; to which the learned Sarnelli adds: "As to the name, Berenicia, which we call Veronica, it means the same person whom people honour and invoke in all sickness from the flow of blood, in very many places in France." Although, in changing the name, instead of Berenicia, or Veronica, they say in some places, Venizia. in others, Veniza, it is evi-

dent from the paintings, that this is the very
same saint, for she is always represented as
having at her side the towel, or handkerchief,
on which is represented the Holy Face, as a
distinctive mark, as Bollandus truly observes
in his "Historical Commentaries of St.
Veronica."

As to the question of knowing if the
name *Veronica* (which is said to be composed of the Latin word *Vera*, true, and a
Greek word Latinized *icon*, an image, i.e. true
image,) is a name predestined or symbolical,
as those of Christopher Columbus,* and
Mezzofanti,† or rather if the name be one
by inheritance to the saint, from the desig-
nation of the towel, it is not repugnant to
believe that this holy woman, chosen by Almighty God for so exalted an action, had
likewise received from Providence a prophetic
name. Moreover, it must be kept in mind that
the name Berenicia, which she is generally

* The name Christophorus Columbus recalls to our mind
the dove going from the ark and bringing back to Noe the
olive branch, the symbol of peace, as also the cross which the
great navigator planted in the New World, which he went to
discover to sow the faith of Jesus Christ.

† The name is composed of the Italian "*mezzo*" and Latin
"*fans*" (part. of fari) speaking. It is known that the illustrious cardinal spoke more than fifty languages.

called, and which the Greeks have adopted,
is the same in meaning as Veronica, which
the Latins employ. The Latins change the
Greek consonant B into V, so of Berenicia
they easily make Veronica.*   In the mean-

---

* The Macedonians explain Pheronica as *ferens victoriam*
bearing away the victory. The Latins employed F in place of
the consonant V, from the time of the Emperor Claudius, who,
to distinguish the consonant V from the vowel V, introduced
the Eolian digamma, a letter or figure composed of two
Greek gammas, superposed, and forming our capital F ; so
for *Servus* or *civis* they wrote SerFus and ciFis. Pliny, lib.
7, c. 41, calls *Pheronica* what Valerius Maximus lib. 8, calls
Berenicia: " cui soli ex mulieribus, quod filia, mater et
soror esset Olympionicarum concessum est ut gymnicos
ludos posset spectare, foeminis omnibus interdictos."

The circumstances which accompany the gift of this holy
image by our Saviour, as well as the considerations above,
fully justify the natural etymology of the name Veronica
which is from the words *Vero* (abl. de verum, i) *by the truth*,
and *Nica, be a conqueror.* Jesus is the *truth*, and died to
destroy the empire of the devil, that He might leave to His
Church, in the person of His faithful servant, this pledge of
His eternal love, which the name (Sols vainqueur par la
Vérité) as a glorious device opposed to the war-cry of His
enemies in every age: " Montez, montez, toujours." Jesus
is the Word made flesh, and at the same time the truth ; and if
we have recourse to anagrams, the name Veronica represents
to us the divinity by the vowels A E I O V, which compose
the name JEOVA, and His humanity by the consonants
R. N. C., which are the initials of the three titles given to
Him as man ; *Rex, Nazarenus, Christus.* King, Nazarean,
Christ. "In the beginning was the Word, and the Word
was with God, and the Word was God ; and the Word was made
flesh, and dwelt amongst us."—St. John. And as the true
cross was distinguished from the others by the miracles it
wrought, so the Veronica daily proves its authenticity by the

time we are inclined to believe, with a great
number of authors, that Veronica was the
name first given to the holy towel on which
was impressed the real likeness of our Saviour, and that by degrees the faithful gave
this name to the holy woman who is represented in pictures or paintings holding the
holy towel in her hands. It is likewise true
that authors call the holy Face itself Veronica, and that in the time of Innocent III.
medals were cast with the image of the holy
Face on them, which were called Veronicas,
and those who sold them were called *vendors
of Veronicas*, and likewise in the old Missals
of some of the dioceses in Germany, especially those of the church of Augsburg,
(Augusta Vindelicorum) printed in 1555, is
to be seen the rubric, "Missa de Vultu sanc-
to seu Veronica"—"Mass of the Holy Face
or Veronica." Giacomo Gretsero* says that
in Germany they have a custom to paint in
the churches, at the right of the high altar,
the image of Veronica, and that the people
have a devotion, as they approach it, to make

graces of every kind which it pours on those who wish to
implore the mercy of Him whom it represents.

* Tract de Imaginibus non manufactis, cap. 7.

the sign of the cross on it, and afterwards on themselves. The practice of this devotion is so frequent that it becomes necessary to renew and refresh these paintings which, by the continuous contact of the hands, lose their colour and become effaced.

Be the name and identity as it may, of this pious woman, who had the happiness of consoling our dear Lord in the midst of His sorrows, we know that she brought to Rome this precious treasure which had been confided to her. It is said that in going to the Eternal City she landed at the isle of Zante, where she planted the faith of Christ. It is for this reason the inhabitants of this island, who received from Veronica the first precepts of the Christian religion honour her memory with a peculiar devotion.

Many important and authentic documents attest the arrival of St. Veronica in the city of Rome. Peter the Deacon, who flourished about the year 515, says : " The towel with which Christ wiped His face, and which some call Veronica, was brought to Rome in the time of Tiberius Cæsar."*

---

* Sudarium cum quo Christus faciem suam extersit, quod ab aliis Veronica dicitur tempore Tiberii Cæsaris Romanis delatum est, et

It is said that Tiberius was cured of a leprosy by the presence alone of the holy Face,
which Veronica exposed in his palace, and
that he was anxious to load her with favours;
but she had received from our Lord a treasure in comparison with which all other
things were as nothing, and she piously
guarded it till her death. Of the two cases or
shrines in which the holy relic was brought
to Rome, the larger one is venerated in the
church of St. Mary of Martyrs, and the other
in the church of S. Eligio de' Ferrari. Alvieri gives us the inscription which was on
the case at St. Mary of the Martyrs, as it
was in his time: " In this case the towel of
the Passion of our Saviour Jesus Christ was
brought from Jerusalem in the time of Tiberius Augustus."*

St. Veronica died at Rome, and the sacred
treasure remained in the possession of Clement I. (fourth successor to St. Peter) who
governed the Church from the year 91 to
100. Pietro Galesino makes mention of it
in his Martyrology, in these words: *Romæ,
S. Veronicæ quæ vultum Domini ad eam*

* In ista capsa fuit portatum Sudarium Passionis Domini
Nostri Jesu-Christi a Hierosolymis Tiberio Auguste

Urbem a Hierosolymis attulit." It is thought
that her body lies buried in the Vatican
Basilica, not far from the Holy Image, which
is an invincible labarum placed over the
City, to defend it against the assaults of the
enemy, and an object of the veneration of
the faithful in every age, and worthy of the
veneration of the whole world.

During the persecutions of the first three
centuries which beat so terribly against the
vessel of the infant Church, Clement and
his successors secretly preserved the holy
relic in the depths of the catacombs; but
when God caused the aurora of a new era of
tranquillity and peace to rise on His Church,
she came forth with these treasures from
these dark dwellings and shone in full day.
Constantine was desirous to build a temple
at the base of the Vatican hill, where St.
Peter was buried. We then behold the hands
of Cæsar, which were formerly employed in
raising temples to idols, now sanctified in
building in that part of Rome, which was
most sullied by Pagan superstitions, and on
the very site of the Temple of Apollo, the
magnificent church of the Fisherman of
Galilee, where future generations should
come to consult the *infallible* oracles of

Truth. This august sanctuary, embellished by the munificence of Constantine and his mother St. Helen, was consecrated by Pope St. Sylvester, on the 18th November, 324. It is in this Basilica, so often enlarged, restored, and completely reconstructed, that the Holy Face was preserved and venerated from time immemorial. If we find it deposited in other churches of Rome as in the Rotunda, Holy Ghost, and in the Castle of St. Angelo, it is only for a time, St. Peter's being situated outside the city, it was more exposed than these already named, and the Roman Pontiffs wishing to have the Holy Relic secure, sent it to them.

In the year 610, during the Pontificate of Boniface IV., the Holy Face was venerated in the church of St. Mary of the Martyrs, commonly called the Rotunda, by reason of its round form. This was the old Pantheon, built by Agrippa to Jupiter the Avenger, and later dedicated to all the Olympic deities. In the year of our Lord 608, Boniface IV., wishing to purify this temple, and to dedicate it to the Mother of God, went into the catacombs, and brought forth from their subterranean habitations a legion of Christian heroes, and sent them in twenty-

eight magnificently decorated carriages,
amidst the acclamations of all Rome, into
the sanctuary of vanquished Paganism. The
new church got the name of St. Mary of the
Martyrs. Two centuries later, in 830, Gregory IV. consecrated it again to All the
Saints, and commanded that, in memory of
this consecration, there should be celebrated
every year, and on the 1st November, in
the entire Catholic world, the Feast of All
Saints.

He wished to give St. Mary of the Martyrs
the charge of the holy relic, being a place
well fortified and very safe, and being likewise situated almost in the centre of the
city, and at the same time sufficiently large
to accommodate the multitudes of people
who would go there to offer their adoration
to our Saviour.

They have, even in our time, in this
church, the case or shrine where the Holy Face
was preserved. The urn which contained this
case is placed in pieces on the table of the
altar of the holy crucifix, with the following
inscription: "*Arca in qua sacrum sudarium,
olim a diva Veronica delatum Romam ex
Palestina, hac in Basilica, annis centum
enituit.*"—"The case in which the Holy

Towel brought from Palestine by Blessed Veronica, was kept with honour in this Basilica for a hundred years." This case or shrine had ten locks, the keys of which were entrusted to the care of the chiefs of the ten old *Rioni*, or Roman regions, so that the holy Relic was committed to the care of the entire city, and its case could only be opened before its united representatives.

The holy Relic was exposed to the veneration of the faithful once a year, May 13, the anniversary of the first consecration of the church, as also in days of calamity, to invoke the pardon and protection of God.

A century later the Holy Face was brought to St. Peter's. Pope John VII., in the year 707, having built an oratory in the Vatican Basilica, which he dedicated to the Blessed Virgin *"del Presepio,"* and in which he wished to have his sepulture, raised an altar in it in honour of the Holy Face, (*quod vocatur Veronica*) and placed it there in a beautiful, large, and ornamented tabernacle, with marble pillars, and the chapel took the name, and was called "*Santa Maria del Sudario.*"

Grimaldi, the notary and archivist of the Basilica, says that the altars of this Oratory were consecrated on the 24th November, 707, and that Pope John VII. placed the Holy Relic there on the following day.

Torrigio, in a work of his called "*Sagre Grotte Vaticane*," assigns the same date for the replacing of the Holy Relic in St. Peter's, it having been for some time in the Rotunda or church of *St. Mary of the Martyrs*.

He also says that, under Adrian I., the tabernacle was enlarged, and surrounded by a balcony from which the Holy Face was exposed to the people for veneration.

P. Mabillon, in his *Museum Italicum*, vol. ii., p. 122, inserts a Roman Ceremonial of 1130, dedicated to Cardinal Guy du Chatal, later Celestine II., where it is said, "afterwards the Pontiff goes to the *Towel* of Christ, which is called Veronica, and incenses it."

Alvieri affirms, with other authors, that in the time of Innocent II. six noble Roman families were appointed to guard the Holy Face, and to take care of the case or shrine in which it was enclosed.

Mallio, in his History of Remarkable Things in the Vatican Basilica, dedicated to Alexander III. in 1159, attests the remarkable veneration which was given to the Holy

Face during this epoch, before which burned day and night *ten* lamps. (*Ante Veronicam decem lampades die noctuque.*)

We have already spoken of the medals called Veronicas, which had impressed on them the likeness of the Holy Face, and the keys of St. Peter. The pilgrims to the tombs of the apostles, who had great confidence in the holy relic, attached them to their clothes.

Such was the veneration given to the Holy Image that it was often represented on the Pontifical coins. Scilla, in his treatise, *Delle Monete Pontificie*, shews different sorts of these coins, with the likeness of the Holy Face struck on them.

Cancellieri says that Philip Augustus, King of France, being come to Rome in 1193, Pope Celestine III. showed him " The Veronica; that is to say, a certain linen which Jesus Christ applied to His Face, and which remains so manifestly imprinted even to this day, that you would believe you see the Face itself of Jesus Christ. They call it Veronica, from the name of the woman to whom the linen belonged, whose name was Veronica."

Innocent III., who filled the chair of St

Peter in 1198, had a great veneration for the
Holy Face; he composed some prayers in
its honour, ordered them to be recited before
it, and attached to them certain indulgences.
Cancellieri, without specifying the date,
says that the Holy Face was transferred to
the hospital of the Holy Ghost; he mentions
an old chronicle, from which it appears that
the holy towel was at the house of *S. Spirito
in Sassia*, in a little chamber entirely made of
iron and marble, secured with six locks and
keys, which were confided to six Roman
families. It was exposed only once a year,
and the gentlemen who had the honour of
holding the keys, enjoyed the Franchise;
they were not bound to do any civil service,
and if one of them were appointed to be a
senechal, &c., he was not obliged to do so.
Each time that the holy relic was shown,
they should be present, each with twenty
companions, all armed around the holy
image, to accompany it to the place appointed,
and secure it. It was probably in memory
of this temporary guard of the Holy Face in
the church of the Holy Ghost, that Pope
Innocent III. instituted by a bull, in 1208,
the procession which was usually made every
year on the first Sunday after the Octave

of the Epiphany, and in which was solemnly borne the Holy Face, from the Vatican Basilica to the church of the Holy Ghost. They likewise distributed a great amount of alms to poor strangers and to hospitals. The holy relic remained some time in the church of the Holy Ghost, and was afterwards brought back again to the Vatican Basilica. Later, about the year 1471, Sixtus IV., for just motives, abolished this procession, and decreed that instead the people should go every year, on the same day, to venerate the Relic in the Vatican Basilica. The members of the Archconfraternity of St. Peter, in Sassia, which existed in 1198, and which had the honour to guard, for some time, the Holy Relic, having undoubtedly succeeded the six gentlemen already mentioned, now formed the procession to St. Peter's, on the second Sunday after the Epiphany, also on Whit-Monday, and, by a privilege, had an exposition of the Holy Face, which exposition was also made three times a year to the foundlings of both sexes, and to the ecclesiastics of the hospital of the Holy Ghost, in remembrance of the time it was formerly kept there.

Boniface VIII. re-established in 1300, at

Rome, the celebration of the "Holy Year," in the midst of an immense concourse of people, who came to Rome to gain the plenary indulgence. For the consolation of the pilgrims, he exposed the Holy Face every Friday and on solemn feasts. The same Pope exposed it to Charles II., King of Sicily, and James II., King of Aragon.

Rinaldi informs us, that in the year 1328, at the time when Louis of Bavaria, with his heretics and schismatics, and a number of courtiers, came to Rome, the city was interdicted, and many of the Faithful, as also many ecclesiastics and religious fled. The canon of St. Peter's, who had charge of the holy towel, concealed it, because this crowd of atheists were not worthy to behold it.

Clement VI., residing at Avignon, issued an order to celebrate at Rome, in 1350, the second General Jubilee. It is impossible to conceive the great concourse of pilgrims on this occasion; the crowd was so great, that, many times, numbers of the people died, as Matteo Villani, who was present, testifies. The Pope wrote to the canons of the Vatican, ordering them to have many expositions of the Holy Face, on account of the great devotion of the people for this Holy Relic.

Louis I., King of Hungary, asked, and obtained permission of the Sovereign Pontiff, to venerate it every day.

Cancellieri, in his work, " *Settimana Santa*," says that the Holy Face was brought to the Castle of St. Angelo, as appears from an old journal, which says: "The 4th of October, 1409, the towel of St. Veronica was brought from the sacristy of St. Peter's to the Castle of St. Angelo, where it might be safe from the insults of the soldiers."[*]

A contemporary journalist, Antonio de Pietri, adds : "January 1, 1410, at the hour of *Tierce, Jacomo de Calvi*, canon, vicar and sacristan of the Basilica of St. Peter, accompanied by six other canons, went to the castle of San-Angelo, and brought from it to St. Peter's the Veronica, or Holy Face."

Nicholas, in 1450, had three little bells made, with silvery and harmonious sounds, to announce the exposition of the Holy Relic, as is the practice at this present time. On the bells was the following inscription, "*Nicolaus Papa V. fecit anno Jubilæi 1450.*"

---

[*] Ladislaus, King of Naples, taking advantage of the schism, occupied Rome, whence Paolo Orsini drove him in December 1407.

During this "*Holy Year*," the multitudes of pilgrims, having recourse to venerate the Holy Relic, were so great that, in one day alone, eighty-seven persons fell from the bridge of San Angelo, into the Tiber, and were drowned.

We know from Torrigio, that Nicholas V., in 1452, after having crowned the Emperor, Frederic III., and created him Canon of the Vatican, as was customary, gave him the special power, in canonical costume, to expose in the tabernacle the Holy Face, and to venerate with awe and respect the Holy Relic, a favour not usually accorded even to the beneficed canons. It is necessary here to remember that the emperors, after their coronation by the Pope, became canons of the chapters of the Lateran, and the Vatican, and wore the rochet, cope, and biretta. The emperors who wished to venerate the Holy Relic, through devotion, were obliged to do so in canonical costume.

The Emperor of Turkey having made a present to Innocent VIII., of the holy lance, which pierced the side of our Redeemer, the Pope kept it in his room, intending to build a sumptuous chapel for it, in the Basilica of St. Peter; but, finding his end approach,

.he ordered that the Relic should be placed in the chapel of the Holy Face.

It was during the pontificate of Urban VIII., in 1625, that the Holy Face was solemnly borne into the new Basilica of St. Peter, on its completion, and placed in the niche where it is venerated at the present day. For a long time, the old church, built by Constantine, threatening decay, Pope Nicholas V. the great protector of letters and of arts, conceived the design of raising around the old Basilica, a temple sufficiently large to represent by its form the universal Church. The labours commenced in 1450. Julius II., admirably assisted by Bramanta, forwarded the execution by the energy and ardour of his resolute character; after him, Leo X. and Raphael continued the work, without interruption. Michael Angelo laboured during seventeen years, under five successive Popes. This great man, in a moment of sublime inspiration, taking on the wings of his genius, the Pantheon, the greatest work of ancient art, had borne it into the air to the height of 300 feet, on four enormous pillars of pentagonal form, afterwards raising the crown-work of the papal altar, the cupola of St. Peter's, that sublime cupola which pilgrims hail in the distance, with tears in their eyes, and which cannot be thought of without emotion, by any one who has had the happiness to behold it.

Urban VIII., on his elevation to the papal throne, found this great work very near completion, and gave a great impetus to it. He ordered Bernin to make in the pillars of the admirable cupola the four niches, with places for the exposition of the holy relics, and, on the 23rd December, 1625, the Holy Face and the Holy Lance, which had been previously deposited in the archives of the Basilica, and enclosed in a case, or shrine, of iron, covered with rich cloth, were borne in a procession, under a canopy, to a niche, since called the "Holy Veronica." The canopy was carried on the occasion by the Archduke Leopold, son of the Emperor Ferdinand III., and by other great personages.

To add to the splendour of the basilica and increase more and more the veneration of the faithful, Urban VIII, on the 8th of April 1629, wished to add to the image of the Holy Face and Holy Lance, the wood of the true cross, and commanded by a bull, that the three Relics should be always ex-

posed one after the other, he likewise granted
a plenary indulgence to those, who, having
confessed and worthily communicated, should
be present at the exposition. Urban VIII.
extended it to the following day, to the
twentieth hour, (about two o'clock in the
afternoon,) and prostrate before the holy
Relics, he venerated them with great devotion, and commanded under pain of excommunication, by a notice which he placed
under the niche, that no one should remove
the veil which covers the Holy Face, without
the authority of the Pope.

We should mention here the arrival at
Rome in 1625 of Wladeslas, son of Sigis-
mond III, King of Poland, who was received
by Urban VIII, and presented with the cloak
and blest sword in recompense for his valo-
rous devotion to the Church. By a special
favour, the Pope created him a Canon of St.
Peter's, in order that he might be able to
venerate, near at hand, the Holy Face. The
prince approached the tabernacle in surplice
and rochet, but without a stole, because he
was not in Holy Orders, and was authorized
to show to the people the Holy Relic with
the assistance of two other canons. Devenu,
King of Poland in 1632, under the name of

Wladislas VII, received from the chaplain
and canons of St. Peter's a letter of con-
gratulation, to which he made the following
beautiful reply :—" We have not forgotten
that, during our sojourn in Rome, we were
added to your college, to the end that we
might contemplate the Holy Face of our
Saviour."

The pious Como, grand Duke of Tuscany,
having come to Rome in 1700 to gain the indulgence of the general Jubilee, and to venerate the Holy Face, Innocent XII. created
him a canon in order that he might be able to
hold in his hands the holy Relics.   He went
to the shrine clothed in a violet soutane,
wearing surplice, biretta and red gloves, according to the custom even in our days, and
after having devoutly venerated the Holy
Relic, he exposed it to the people and stand-
ing between two canons blessed them with it.
A painting in the Vatican represents him
dressed as a canon.

By a brief " *Ut carrissimus*," of 31st. May,
1717, Clement XI. granted to James III. of
England, (commonly called the *Pretender*,
son of James II.) the privilege of venerating
the Holy Face in the Vestibule of the oratory
where it is religiously preserved.

Pius VII. of happy memory, granted that Charles Emmanuel IV. King of Sardinia, afterwards a Jesuit, and the Queen his wife, the Venerable Mary Clotilda of France, should have the consolation of beholding and kissing the Holy Face of our Saviour in the Vestibule of the Sanctuary. If the present representative of this illustrious House of Savoy, this family of Saints, had not repudiated the inheritance of piety which was left him by his ancestors, he would not have caused so much sorrow to the Church, and so many tears to our glorious and beloved Pontiff, Pius IX.

Pius VII. granted a special favour in February 1801, to the pious Archduchess Maria Anne of Austria, who came to receive the most Adorable Eucharist in the Basilica. After having satisfied her devotion, the Canons blest with the Holy Relic, the court, and the people assembled in the temple.

April 7, 1806, the same pope, after the ceremonies of the Monday of the Passover, went with his noble court to the Vatican Basilica; then preceded by lighted torches, assisted by two canons, went to the Sanctuary of the Veronica. After having prayed for some time before the three very Holy Relics

3

he allowed also his suite to approach and venerate so glorious a souvenir of our Lord's Redemption.

We had ourselves the consolation (sweet souvenir) of assisting in 1853 at an exposition of the Holy Face, made before our Most Holy Father Pius IX. On Friday at 10 o'clock, A. M., the pope arrived at the Vatican Basilica; after having adored our Saviour in the chapel of the Most Holy Sacrament, he proceeded with his court to the confessional of St. Peter, and knelt down at the tomb of the glorious Apostles. A canon robed in the costume already described ascended to the Relics, took in his hands successively the Holy Lance, the blessed wood of the Cross, and that of the Holy Face of our Lord and Saviour Jesus Christ. Pius IX. the Cardinals and the faithful, prostrated on the floor of the temple, gazed upon, and lovingly bowed under the benediction which he gave them. After having satisfied his devotion, Pius IX. returned to his palace, but not without having first, at the foot of the fisherman, bowed his venerable head, where shone the triple crown of priesthood, sanctity, and martyrdom.

The following year 1854, a year ever

memorable on account of the dogmatic
definition of the Immaculate Conception of
the Blessed Virgin Mary, Cardinal Patrizzi,
Vicar of Rome, announced in the " *Invito
Sagro,*" of the 28th of November, that by
order of the Holy Father, the three great
Relics would be exposed on an altar of the
Basilica of St. Peter, the first Sunday of
Advent, December the 3rd, and that they
would remain exposed till the noon of the
Thursday following. The Holy Face and the
two other Relics were placed on the altar of
the Most Holy Sacrament, under a canopy,
in order that as great a number as possi-
ble of the bishops who had come to Rome
for this solemn occasion, should have the
consolation of celebrating there, the Holy
Mysteries. It was the first time that the
Holy Face was exposed for so many days
on an altar in the Vatican Basilica; the
Pope wished to signify by this extraordinary
favour, the glorious promulgation of the
great privilege of our glorious Mother, which
was desired for the last eighteen centuries,
and which excited so much joy in heaven
and on earth. Thus is preserved from the
commencement of the Church to the present
time, the most Holy Relic of our Lord Jes

Christ, since His Divine Body ascended into heaven. Since the time that Veronica received from the blessed hands of our Saviour, this everlasting pledge of His love, to the time when she gave it to Pope Clement I. the fourth successor of St. Peter to Pius IX. now gloriously reigning, this image of our Lord has not ceased to be under the guardianship and in the hands of the sovereign Pontiffs. And although the city of Rome had been often pillaged and sacked, Divine Providence did not permit sacrilegious hands to defile this Holy Relic. All the popes have watched it with a jealous care, and guarded it with love and veneration; many composed hymns and prayers in its honour, which are sung in the religious ceremonies. (see p. 52.)

We behold from time to time illustrious princes, kings and renowned emperors making pilgrimages to Rome, to contemplate the adorable features of our Saviour in His dolorous Passion; we see them lay down their sceptres and crowns, and despoil themselves of their high birth, to venerate on their knees and in tears, the linen all covered with sweat and blood where the divine features were represented, esteeming

these holy vestiges more than all the master-
pieces of art and all the other treasures
which are accumulated in Rome, and appre-
ciating their own dignities inasmuch as they
procured for them the exceptional favour of
beholding more closely this venerable Relic
of our Saviour.

The people hastened often in crowds,' and
exposed themselves to every fatigue and peril,
and even looked upon themselves as happy
when permitted to venerate even in the distance, the Holy Face. In the years of the
general jubilees, and in times of great
calamities, the people hurried to the holy
Relic as to a powerful Palladium, and cried
out, "Lord, show us Thy Face, and we shall
be saved,"—(" Domine ostende faciem tuam,
et salvi erimus.") Ps. lxxix. 8. They would
strike their breasts and shed abundant tears,
when they considered the lamentable state
into which their sins had reduced the Redeemer, and entering into themselves, their
hearts would be filled with consolation and
hope. Often in these circumstances, God
displayed His mercy by great miracles, and
granted singular favours for this great devotion of the people towards the Holy Face.

The Church always guarded this precious

treasure with a jealous care, we were going to say parsimoniously. It was only at rare intervals that the popes consented to raise the veil which covered the Holy Image, and the archives of the Vatican preserve the ... which granted this rare favour to some ... princes. The sovereign Pontiffs ordinarily keep in their possession, one of the keys of the Sanctuary which surrounds this Divine Jewel, and it was prohibited under pain of excommunication to go near it without their authority. It was only shown once or twice each year to the faithful.

It was likewise prohibited under pain of excommunication to reproduce by painting the Holy Image, and we only know of two authentic copies which have been made in times past. One sent in 1249, to the Abbey of *Montreuil les Dames, in Tierache* by James of Troyes, then chaplain to Innocent IV. and later Urban IV., which is at present venerated in the Church of Notre Dame de Laon;* the other given by Gregory XV. in 1621, to a lady of the family of Sforza, who

* The Feast of the Holy Face is celebrated at Notre Dame de Laon, on the Sunday after the octave of SS. Peter and Paul with an *immense* concourse of pilgrims.

gave it to the professed house of the Jesuits at Rome, where it is at present.

The sovereign Pontiffs appear to have departed a little in these times from their primitive severity. They have allowed to be exposed in different churches of the Catholic world, faithful and authentic reproductions* of the Holy Face at Rome, in order to rekindle in the hearts of men, faith and piety almost extinct. We live in an age of coldness and indifference: men are confused by materialism, which dries up the heart and stifles in the soul every germ of religion. "Impiety, corruption of morals, unbridled passions, the contagion of wicked opinions of every sort, all the vices and crimes, the violation of divine and human laws,† are everywhere propagated, and to

* The copies are printed on linen, or cotton, or silk, white or red, with the sealed stamp of the metropolitan Canon who guards it, accompanied by a letter of its authenticity.

† The habit of blasphemy and the violation of the Sunday so common in our days, are wicked outrages against the Holy Face of our Divine Saviour. This is why there are formed in many towns, " Reparative associations" of pious persons, who endeavour, as " new Veronicas," to wipe devoutly by their veneration and their love, the disfigured features of the Redeemer, and merit that our Saviour, in recompense, would impress His Divine Image on their souls. Our Saviour has revealed this devotion to many religious who died in the odour of sanctity, and his Vicar on earth, Pius IX. has said : " Reparation is a divine work destined to save society."

such an extent that not only our holy religion, but even human society are miserably in trouble and confusion."*

Then nothing is more suitable to stop this torrent of corruption which threatens to draw away by force the entire world than the sight of the Holy Face of our Redeemer. In all places where this devotion is established, piety is enkindled in the souls of men, and with it the love of their neighbour, sweetness, humility, resignation in sufferings, every virtue, in a word, of which our Saviour has given us an example in His Passion. We likewise know that in honouring the Image of our Saviour we honour Himself of whom that Image reminds us; this is why God was pleased to bless this devotion, and make shine forth the wonderful effects of His almighty and holy *goodness*.

The expositions of the Holy Face in the Vatican Basilica are also more frequent than formerly. They are on the following days:

The Second Sunday after the Epiphany

---

* The Apostolic letter of our holy Father, Pius IX., convoking the Œcumenical Council on the Feast of the Immaculate conception, 1869.

and Whit-Monday, for the brothers of the Arch-Confraternity of the Holy Ghost.

Wednesday of Holy Week, after the Tenebræ.

Many times during Thursday and Friday of the same week.

Holy Saturday, in the morning after Mass.

Easter Sunday, after the ceremonies, for the Pope, Cardinals, and other persons who took part in them.

The following Monday, before and after Vespers, together with the other relics of the Basilica.

Ascension-day, after Mass.

The 3rd May, the Feast of the Invention of the Holy Cross.

The 18th November, the anniversary of the Dedication of the Basilica of St. Peter.

The 18th January, the Feast of the Chair of St. Peter at Rome.

The 22nd February, the Feast of the Chair of St. Peter at Antioch.

Besides, during the calamities of the Church, as in those of Rome, or the Sovereignty of the Holy See, in times of war, earthquakes, pestilence, the overflowing of the Tiber, &c., the Popes expose the Holy Face and the other great relics; likewise in extraordinary jubilees; penitential processions, and also to implore the divine mercy and heavenly assistance.

When the exposition is made in the presence of the Pope, the blessing is not given from the middle but from the side, in respect for the pontifical majesty. *"In majestatis pontificiæ reverentiam."*

The edifice which encloses the Holy Relics is exteriorly ornamented by a bas-relief representing the Holy Face; below, placed on a base in a large niche, is the colossal statue in marble of St. Veronica, whom Mochi has represented as holding in her hands the Holy Face. A door situated at the foot of this statue, opens an entrance to a passage by which you ascend to the niche where are deposited the Holy Relics, and in descending some steps, you enter into what are called the holy Vatican Grottoes. It is in these Grottoes that the bodies of SS. Peter and Paul are; the tombs of a great number of Popes, whose mausoleums are above in the new Basilica; there also are the four subterranean chapels, which, by order of Urban VIII. Bernice formed in the interior of the pillars which support the cupola. He decorated them with marble

columns of the Ionic order, and placed on
he altar pictures in mosaic of great price.

The picture of the altar of the Holy Face
epresents Veronica presenting the towel or
eil to the Redeemer. On the walls we see,
wo by two, the Holy Virgin and the three
Marys. In the first oval arch, Urban VIII.
s represented as receiving the design of the
our chapels; in the second, Boniface VIII.
xposes the Holy Face to Charles II. King
of Sicily, and James II. King of Aragon, in
296; the third represents the exposition
made by order of Nicholas V. to the Empe-
or Frederic III.

On the walls of the corridor, on the Gos-
el side, is seen St. Veronica presenting
he towel or veil to our Saviour; on the
ides, Martha and Magdalen, opposite St.
Veronica, preparing to set out for Rome
ith the holy Relic; on the sides, Mary
he Mother of James, and Mary Salome, the
irgin Mary, and Mary of Cleophas.

The paintings in the arches represent, 1st,
St. Veronica showing the holy towel to the
eople; 2nd, John VII. with the tabernacle
onstructed by his piety to preserve the holy
Relic; and 3rd, the holy Image shewn to

Lewis I., King of Hungary, by order of Pope Clement VI.

If, instead of descending to the holy Grottoes, you wish to go where the exposition takes place, you open a metal door, and, to your left, you ascend by a winding stair to the sanctuary of the holy Relics. They are laid on a credence, enclosed in a closet or niche, which has three locks, the keys of which are confided to the canons who have charge of the holy Relics. The Holy Face is placed in a distinct reliquary, made with a magnificent crystal frame, silver plated, given the 6th of May, 1350, by three gentlemen of Venice, whose names are preserved in an old registry of the benefactors of the Basilica.

By a remarkable coincidence, another Venetian, Gregory XVI., with his usual forethought, in 1838, substituted, instead of the thin veil which covered the Relic, a plate of crystal, behind which it can be more easily preserved and admired.

The appearance of this holy Image is sufficient to show us the likeness of our divine Saviour; and the innumerable miracles which are performed, also the great veneration in which it has been held in every age, are sufficient to prove the truth of the Catholic tradition.*

Piazza, in his "*Emerologio di Roma*," on the 4th of February, after having given the history of the Holy Face, as we have told it, gives a description of the Holy Face of Rome, in 1713, which was confirmed by Gio-Gregorio, lib. 17, *du Pretoire de Pilate.*

"We there behold, not without being moved by a profound sentiment of compunction, the head of our Saviour pierced by a crown of sharp thorns, the face covered with blood; the eyes swollen and full of blood, the countenance dark and livid; on the right cheek, as well as the bruises, we behold the mark of the gauntlet of Malchus,† who so cruelly struck Him in the house of Anna, and on the other cheek, many spots of spittle; the nose is bruised and bloody, the mouth open and full of

---

* Giacomo Pamelio, in his annotations on Chapter XII. of the Apology of Tertullian, says : "Effigies christi quam Veronicæ in Sudario dedisse traditio est, etiam nunc exstat tanta in veneratione, ut illa dubitare posthac non modo miracula non permittant sed neo aspectus ipse."

† Giovanni Lanspergio, Hom. 19, De Passione, writes; "Quod Christ facies in eodem impressa Sudario digitorum vestiga impressa retineat, et aspicientibus monstrat, quod amata manu Christo Domino infixere."

blood, the teeth are loose, the beard and hair plucked off in many places."

We have compared this description with the copy which we have the happiness to possess in our chapel, and find in it all these characters of resemblance.

So changed, the Divine Face of our Saviour nevertheless presents a mixture of grandeur, compassion, love, and sorrow, which vividly impresses all those who behold it. Under these bruises and spittle, the Christian soul recognizes the majesty of his God, and is moved to repentance at the view of this bloody expiation of his ingratitude, and the soul abandons itself without reserve to a sweet confidence and an ardent love for its Most Blessed Redeemer.

PRAYERS*

FOR THE

VISITS TO THE MOST HOLY TOWEL

OF THE

BLESSED VERONICA.

---

* The Latin texts, the source of which are not given, are taken from a little work called "Indulgenza della Basilica Vaticana."—Roma, 1864.

SACRED HEART OF JESUS,

Purify us,

Sanctify us,

Save us.

AUTHENTIC.

SACROSANCTÆ BASILICÆ
PRINCIPIS APOSTOLORUM DE URBE
CANONICUS.

Universis præsentes litteras inspecturis fidem facio, ac testor me Imaginem Vultus *Domini Nostri* Jesu Christi, ad instar Sanctissimi-Sudarii Veronicæ in tela albi coloris impressam, altitudinis ... unciarum, latitudinis ... unc., reverenter applicasse eidem Sudario, nec non Ligno vivificæ Crucis et Lanceæ Dominicæ cuspidi, quæ in prædicta nostra Basilica religiosissime asservantur, ac pluribus Summorum Pontificum Diplomatibus, maximaque populorum veneratione celebrantur. In quorum fidem prædictam Imaginem et has præsentes litteras meo sigillo obsignavi, et subscripsi.

Datum ex ædibus meis, die 21 Junii MDCCCLXVI. Indictione Rom...... 9. Pontificatus Smi D. N. Domini, Pii Papæ IX. Pont. Max. anno XXI.

(L. S.)   A. THEODOLI.

4

THE CANON

"I certify and attest to all those who will see
these presents, that an Image of the Face of our
Lord and Saviour Jesus Christ, in imitation of
the most holy Towel of Veronica, impressed on
white linen of ... inches high, and of ... inches
broad, has been respectfully applied to the same
Towel, as also to the wood of the vivifying Cross,
and to the iron of the Lance of our Saviour, which
are most religiously preserved in our above-men-
tioned Basilica, and rendered remarkable by
many diplomas of the Sovereign Pontiffs, and
the great veneration of the people. In faith of
which I have subscribed and signed with my seal
the above named image and these presents.

"Given at my residence, the 21 June, in the
year of our Lord 1866.

"Roman Indiction 9, and xxi year of the Pontificate of our Most Holy Father Pope Pius IX.

(Place of Seal.)   "A. THEODOLI."

VERA EFFIGIES
sacri Vultus D. N. Jesu Christi.
quæ Romæ in sacrosancta basilica
S. Petri in Vaticano,
religiosissime asservatur et colitur.

O Lord Jesus! at the sight of Your Most Holy Face, disfigured by sorrow, at the sight of Your Sacred Heart, so full of love, I cry out with St. Augustine: "Lord Jesus, sink deep into my heart Your Sacred Wounds, so that I may read therein Your sorrow and Your love, Your sorrow to endure every sorrow for You, Your love, to despise every love for You."

"Scribe, Domine Jesu, vulnera tua in corde meo, ut in eis legam dolorem et amorem: dolorem, ad sustinendum pro te omnem dolorem ; amorem, ad contemnendum pro te omnem amorem."—S. Augustinus.

RHYTHMUS.

Salve, sancta Facies nostri Redemptoris,*
  In qua nitet species divini decoris,
  Impressa panniculo nivei candoris
  Dataque Veronicæ signum ob amoris.

Salve, decus sæculi, speculum sanctorum,
  Quod videre cupiunt spiritus cœlorum,
  Nos ab omni macula purga vitiorum,
  Atque nos consortio junge beatorum.

Salve, vultus Domini, imago beata,
  Ex æterno munere mire decorata,
  Lumen funde cordibus ex vi tibi data,
  Et a nostris sensibus tolle colligata.

Salve, robur fidei nostræ christianæ,
  Destruens hæreticos, qui sunt mentis vanæ,
  Horum auge meritum qui te credunt sane,
  Illius effigiem qui rex fit ex pane.

Salve, nostrum gaudium in hac vita dura,
  Labili et fragili cito peritura,
  Nos educ ad propria, O felix figura,
  Ad videndam faciem quæ est Christi pura.

---

* Pope John XXII. who was raised to the popedom in 1816 at Avignon, composed this prayer in honour of the Holy Relic, and granted an indulgence of 25 years and as many quarantines to any one who should say it. He granted the

HYMN.

Hail! O blessed Face of our Redeemer,
Where shines celestial splendour,
Upon linen white divinely impressed,
A pledge of love to Veronica blest.

Hail! world's glory, mirror of the skies,
To whom both Thrones and Powers raise their
eyes,
Our vices and our sins, O Lord, wipe away,
And grant to us the bliss of Your eternal day

Hail, O blessed Face of our Saviour,
Down from on high grant us this favour,
Let one seraphic flame to us be given,
That hearts from earth may soar up to heaven.

Hail! of our faith the giver and keeper,
Destroyer of schism and unbeliever,
Lord, increase and bless the just who incline
Before the image of Your Face Divine.

Hail, joy of our life, as through perils we go,
Be our defender from th' infernal foe;
On the wings of the wind waft us through space,
To the realms of joy to gaze on Thy Face.

same indulgence to all those who cannot read it, but who
should say for the same intention five our Fathers, and five
Hail Marys, and Glory be to the Father, &c.

Salve, gemma nobilis, divina margarita,
　Cœlicis virtutibus perfecte munita,
　Non depicta manibus, sculpta vel polita,
　Hoc fit summus Pontifex, qui te fecit ita.

Ille color cœlicus qui in te splendescit,
　In eodem permanet statu, nec decrescit,
　Diuturno tempore minime pallescit,
　Fecit te rex gloriæ fallere qui nescit.

Nesciens putredinem, servans incorruptum
　Quod est a Christicolo coram te deductum,
　Tu vertis in gaudium gemitum et luctum,
　Confer saluberrimum te videndi fructum.

Esto nobis, quæsumus, scutum et juvamen,
　Dulce refrigerium atque consolamen,
　Ut nobis non noceat hostile gravamen,
　Sed foveamur cœlicum requiem.　Amen.

Oremus.

Lætifica, Domine, vultum familiæ tuæ, et
erue animas nostras ex inferno inferiori, ut tui
vultus contemplatione protecti, carnis desideria
calcare valeamus, et te facie ad faciem venientem
super nos judicem securi videamus, Jesum Christum Dominum nostrum.　Amen.

Hail, divine jewel! diamond so clear!
Whose bright shining flames light the heavenly
    sphere:
God of glory and might You formed it so,
Without the assistance of mortal below.

That colour so bright, which shines far away,
Was always the same, and will ne'er decay,
Time may glide on, but Thou art always new,
Immortal, unchangeable, endlessly true.

O substance immortal, Divine Majesty,
Guard, nourish, and increase our purity;
Dry up our tears, and our sorrows remove,
Bring us to glory to feast on your love.

Be to us, O Lord, a shield of defence,
And preserve by Your grace our innocence,
That when we shall go from this vale of tears,
We may live with You for eternal years. Amen.

Let us pray.

Make glad, O Lord, the face of Thy servant,
and draw our souls from perdition, that, being
protected by the contemplation of Your adorable
Face, we may trample under foot all carnal desires, and behold You without fear, face to face,
when You will come in the clouds of heaven,
with power and majesty to judge us. Through
Christ our Lord. Amen.

RHYTHMUS.

Ave, facies præclara*
  Quæ pro nobis in crucis ara,
  Es facta sic pallida,
  Anxietate denigrata,
  Sudore sanguineo rigata,
  Te texit linteola.

In quo mansit tua forma,
  Quæ passionis norma,
  Est cunctis perlucida.
  Cordi meo sic impressa,
  Per te, Jesu, neque cessa
  Hoc cremare indefessa
  Tui amoris facula.

Post hanc vitam cum beatis,
  Contemplari voluptatis
  Possim vultum deitatis
  In perenni gloria. Amen.

℣. Signatum est super nos lumen vultis tui, Domine.

℟. Dedisti lætitiam in corde meo.

℣. Salvum fac servum tuum.

℟. Deus meus, sperantem in te.

℣. Salvum me fac in misericordia tua, Domine.

℟. Non confundar, quoniam invocavi te.

* This prayer was composed by Clement VI., who granted one hundred days indulgence to those who should recite it before the Holy *Face*.

HYMN.

Hail! glorious Face of the Redeemer,
Which shone on the mount in Godlike splendour
On the Blood-stained altar of Calvary,
Where pale Thou didst grow with anxiety,
Thy Face was all covered with sweat and blood,
Which remained on the towel as on the wood.

As a pledge of Thy ever-blest Passion,
The blest towel retains Thy impression,
As truly now as on that day of grace,
When on the linen You impressed Your Face,
Impress, also, O Lord, deep in my heart,
That grace which to Your beloved You impart.

That when the awful hour of death is near,
When the spirit within me faints for fear,
You may call me with the voice of burning love,
And place me near Thee in the realms above,
With Thy angelic hosts my voice to raise,
In the never-ending hymns of praise. Amen.

℣. O Lord, Thou hast signed upon us the
light of Thy countenance.
℟. Thou hast given joy to my heart.
℣. Save Thy servant.
℟. Who putteth his trust in Thee, my God.
℣. Save me by Thy mercy, O Lord.
℟. That I may not be confounded, since I have
called on Thee.

℣. Illumina faciem tuam super servum tuum.

℟. Et doce me justificationes tuas.

℣. Domine Deus virtutum, converte nos.

℟. Et ostende faciem tuam et salvi erimus.

℣. Domine, exaudi orationem meam.

℟. Et clamor meus ad te veniat.

Oremus.

Deus, qui nobis signatis lumine vultus tui, memoriale tuum instantia Veronicæ imaginem tuam Sudario impressam relinquere voluisti, per passionem et crucem tuam tribue nobis, quæsumus, ita nunc in terris per speculum in ænigmate venerari, adorare, ac honorare te ipsum valeamus, ut te facie ad faciem venientem super nos judicem securi videamus, Dominum nostrum Jesum Christum Filium tuum. Amen.

Omnipotens sempiterne Deus, de cujus munere præeminet hæc facies tua expressa tuo pretioso vultu plebi tuæ, quæ convenit ad hanc recolendam, peccatorum suorum da veniam, et corpus, sermones, sensusque guberna, et actus eorum qui in tua pietate confidunt. Qui vivis et regnas, etc.

℣. Let Thy light shine on Thy servant.

℞. And teach me Thy justifications.

℣. O Lord God of armies, convert us.

℞. Shew us Thy face, and we shall be saved.

℣. Lord, hear my prayer.

℞. And let my supplication come unto Thee.

Let us pray.

O Lord, Who hast shed the light of Thy countenance on us, and Who, by the ministry of Veronica, hast wished to leave us the Image of Thy Holy Face, impressed on this towel, as an everlasting pledge of Thy love, grant us, by Thy Passion and Death, the grace to venerate, adore, and glorify Thee here below, under the veil which conceals Thee from our senses, that we may be able to contemplate Thee without fear, face to face, when Thou wilt come in the clouds of heaven, in power and majesty, to judge us, Jesus Christ our Lord. Amen.

O Eternal and Omnipotent God, Who makest to shine the light of Thy divine Image on Thy people assembled to honour Thee, grant us pardon of our sins, regulate our words, actions, senses, and all the faculties of those who confide in Thy mercy, Who livest and reignest one God, world without end. Amen.

ORATIONES AD SANCTAS RELIQUIAS MAJORES.

AD SANCTUM SUDARIUM BEATÆ VERONICÆ.

Antiph. Tibi dixit cor meum ; Quæsivi vultum
tuum, vultum tuum Domine requiram: ne aver-
tas faciem tuam a me.

℣. Signatum est super nos lumen vultus tui,
Domine.

℞. Dedisti lætitiam in corde meo.

Oremus.

Mentibus nostris, quæsumus Domine, vultus
sancti tui lumen benignus infunde, cujus et sa-
pientia conditi sumus, et providentia guberna-
mur. Per Dominum, etc.

AD SS. CRUCEM DOMINI NOSTRI JESU CHRISTI.

Antiph. O Crux benedicta, quæ sola fuisti
digna portare Regem cœlorum et Dominum.

℣. Dicite in nationibus.

℞. Quia Dominus regnavit a ligno.

Oremus.

Deus, qui unigeniti Filii tui pretioso sanguine
vivificæ Crucis vexillum sanctificare voluisti:
concede quæsumus, eos qui ejusdem sanctæ Crucis gaudent honore, tua quoque ubique protec-
tione gaudere. Per Dominum, etc.

PRAYERS IN PRESENCE OF THE GREATER HOLY RELICS.

Antiphon. My heart has spoken to Thee; my eyes have sought Thee; yes, I will always seek Thy holy Face; do not hide Thy Face from me, do not turn it from Thy servant.

℣. Thou hast signed upon me the light of Thy countenance.

℞. Thou hast given joy to my heart.

Let us pray.

Pour, O Lord, we beseech Thee, the light of Thy holy Face into our souls, Thou, Whose wisdom hast created us, and Whose providence governs us. Through Christ our Lord. Amen.

BEFORE THE MOST HOLY CROSS OF OUR LORD JESUS CHRIST.

Antiphon. O blessed Cross, which alone wast worthy to bear the King and Lord of Heaven.

℣. Proclaim to the Gentiles

℞. That the Lord hath reigned from the Cross.

Let us pray.

O God, Who, by the precious Blood of Thy only Son, wished to sanctify the Standard of the Cross, grant, we beseech Thee, that those who love to venerate this same blessed Cross, may likewise rejoice in Thy powerful protection. Through Christ our Lord. Amen.

AD FERRUM LANCÆ D. N. JESU CHRISTI.

Antiph. Unus militum Lancea latus ejus aperuit, et continuo exivit sanguis et aqua.

℣. Lanceis suis vulneraverunt me.

℞. Et concussa sunt omnia ossa mea.

Oremus.

Deus qui ex tui sacri Corporis latere, per Lanceam militis sanguinem tuum in pretium, et aquam in lavacrum effudisti: concede propitius, ut qui Lanceam ipsam hic veneramur, ab omni hoste ipsius munimine protegamur. Qui vivis et regnas, etc.

ORATIO SANCTI AUGUSTINI.

Ante oculos tuos, Domine, culpas nostras ferimus, et plagas quas accepimus, conferimus.

Si pensamus malum quod fecimus, minus est quod patimur, majus est quod meremur.

Gravius est quod commisimus, levius est quod toleramus.

Peccati poenam sentimus, et peccandi pertinaciam non vitamus.

In flagellis tuis infirmitas nostra teritur, et iniquitas non mutatur.

Mens ægra torquetur, et cervix non flectitur.

Vita in dolore suspirat, et in opere non se emendat.

BEFORE THE HOLY LANCE OF OUR LORD JESUS CHRIST.

Antiphon. One of the soldiers opened His side with a lance, and immediately there issued forth blood and water.

℣. They have wounded Me with their lances.

℟. And all My bones are dislocated.

Let us pray.

O God, Who, from the side of Thy Sacred Body, pierced by the lance of a soldier, poured forth Thy Blood to redeem us, and water to purify us, grant that this same lance, which we here venerate, may protect us always against our enemies. Who livest, &c. Amen.

PRAYER OF ST. AUGUSTINE.

I present myself before Your Face, O my Saviour, loaded with my sins, and the punishments which they have brought on me,

If I consider my iniquities, what I suffer is far below what I have merited.

My sin is greater than my punishment.

Although I resent the just punishment of my faults, I do not abandon committing new ones.

I yield under Your scourges, and I do not become better.

My heart is in affliction, and my obstinacy in sin is always the same.

Si expectas, non corrigimur: si vindicas, non duramus.

Confitemur in correctione, quod egimus: obliviscimur post visitationem quod flevimus.

Si extenderis manum, facienda promittimus: si suspenderis gladium, promissa non solvimus.

Si ferias, clamamus ut parcas: si peperceris, iterum provocamus ut ferias.

Habes, Domine, confitentes reos: novimus quod nisi dimittas, recte nos perimas.

Praesta, Pater omnipotens, sine merito quod rogamus, qui fecisti ex nihilo, qui te rogareut.

Per Christum Dominum nostrum. Amen.

℣. Domine non secundum peccata nostra facias nobis.

℞. Neque secundum iniquitates nostras retribuas nobis.

Oremus.

Deus, qui culpa offenderis, poenitentia placaris, preces populi tui supplicantis propitius respice et flagella tuae iracundiae, quae pro peccatis nostris meremur, averte. Per Christum Dominum nostrum. Amen.

My life passes in misery, and I am not changed.
If You spare me, I change not.
If You strike me, I persevere not.

In the time of affliction I confess my sins with tears, but afterwards I forget very soon my repentance.

When You chastise me I make fervent promises, but if You withhold Your hand I do not keep my contracts.

You strike me, I instantly invoke Your mercy; You pardon me, I provoke again Your anger.

I make to You, O my God, a sincere confession of my sins: I protest in Your presence that if You do not deal with me mercifully, I am in danger of perishing without resource.

Grant me, my Saviour, what I ask of You, though I do not deserve it; since you have made me from nothing, grant me the grace to pray to You. Amen.

℣. Lord, deal not with us according to our sins.

℟. Nor reward us according to our iniquities.

Let us pray.

O God, Who, by sin art offended and by penance pacified, mercifully regard the prayers and supplications of Your people, and turn away the scourges of anger which we deserve for our iniquities. Through Jesus Christ our Lord. Amen.

5

ORATIO AD B. V. MARY.*

Pietate tua, quæsumus Domine, nostro 'm solve vincula peccatorum, et intercedente I .ata semperque Virgine Dei Genitrice Maria, cum beatis Apostolis tuis Petro et Paulo, et omnibus Sanctis, nos famulos tuos et loca nostra, in omni sanctitate custodi, omnes consanguinitate, affinitate, ac familiaritate, nobis conjunctos a vitiis purga, virtutibus illustra, pacem et salutem nobis tribue, hostes visibiles et invisibiles remove, carnalia desideria repelle, aerem salubrem indulge, amicis et inimicis nostris charitatem largire, urbem tuam custodi, Pontificem nostrum *N. N.* conserva, omnes prælatos, principes, cunctumque populum christianum ab omni adversitate custodi, benedictio tua sit super nos semper, et omnibus fidelibus defunctis requiem æternam concede. Per Christum D. N. Amen.

* Leo XII, granted one hundred years indulgence to all the faithful who recite this prayer on Saturday, and forty years only for other days. These two indulgences are not exclusively proper to the Vatican Basilica, as are many others.

PRAYER TO THE B. V. MARY.

O Lord, we beseech Thee to break the chains
of our sins, and by the intercession of the
Blessed and ever Virgin Mary, Mother of God,
and the holy apostles Peter and Paul, and all
the saints, preserve us always in sanctity, Thy
faithful servants and our habitations, cleanse us
from our vices, and enlighten by Thy virtues all
those who are united to us by the ties of blood
and friendship; grant us peace and salvation,
deliver us from our enemies visible and invisible,
banish from our hearts all carnal desires, make
us breathe an air purified from sin, bestow the
treasures of Thy grace on our friends and our
enemies, place a guard on Thy holy city, preserve our beloved Pontiff, *N. N.*, defend from all
evil our prelates, princes, and all Christian people, that Thy blessing may always remain with
us; grant eternal rest to the faithful departed.
Through Jesus Christ our Lord. Amen.

PRAYERS.

O Lord Jesus Christ, in presenting ourselves before Thy Adorable Face, to ask of Thee the graces which we stand most in need of, we beseech Thee, above all, to give us that interior disposition of never refusing at any time to do what Thy holy commandments and precepts demand. Through Christ our Lord. Amen.

O good Jesus, Thou who hast said, "Ask, and you shall receive; seek and you shall find; knock and it shall be opened to you: give us, O Lord, that faith which obtains all, or supply in us what may be deficient; grant us, by the pure effect of Thy charity, the graces which we may stand in need of to gain Thy eternal glory. Through Christ our Lord. Amen.

O Almighty and Eternal God, behold the Face of Thy Son Jesus; we present it to Thee with confidence, to implore Thy pardon. The All-Merciful Advocate opens His mouth to plead our cause, hearken to His cries, behold His tears, O God, and through His infinite merits hearken to Him when He intercedes for us poor and miserable sinners. Amen.

O Adorable Face of my Jesus, so mercifully bowed down on the tree of the Cross, on the day of Thy Passion, for the salvation of the world! to-day again through compassion incline to us poor sinners, let fall on us one look of compassion, and receive us with a kiss of peace. Amen.

Sacred Heart of Jesus, have mercy on us.

Sit nomen Domini benedictum! Amen.

AN ACT OF REPARATION

FOR ALL THE OUTRAGES WHICH JESUS CHRIST HAS SUFFERED IN HIS HOLY FACE.

I adore and praise Thee, O my divine Jesus, Son of the living God, I wish to make Thee satisfaction for all the outrages Thou hast received for me, the most miserable of Thy creatures, in all the members of Thy Blessed Body, and particularly in Thy Adorable Face. Hail Adorable Face, disfigured by blows and sullied by spittle, and hardly recognisable from the cruel treatment which Thou receivedst from the impious Jews. I salute Thee, O blessed Eyes, all bathed in tears, which Thou hast shed for our salvation. I salute Thee, O blessed Ears, annoyed by blasphemies, injuries, and cruel railleries. I salute Thee, blessed Mouth, filled with graces and tenderness for sinners, but filled with vinegar and gall by the monstrous ingratitude of that people whom Thou hadst chosen from all others. In reparation for all these ignominies, I offer Thee all the homage which they give Thee in that holy place where Thou wishest to be honoured with a special worship, in union with them. Amen.

[Abridged from the History of the Holy Face of O. S. J. C., preserved in the Cathedral of Laon.]

AN ACT OF SUBMISSION.

By these words, "Thy sins are forgiven thee," Thou grantedst, O Lord, the remission of the sins of the paralytic, mentioned in the Gospel. Thence I, a miserable sinner, knowing and firmly believing that Thou hast given to Thy priests the power of remitting sins, wish to approach the sacred fount of penance after having besought Thee to look with an eye of mercy on my bodily infirmities. Then, submitting myself both heart and soul to Thy most holy will, O Lord, I will wait in peace the accomplishment of my vows, with the hope of beholding, praising, and blessing Thy Adorable Face for ever and ever. Amen.

HYMNUS.

Vexilla Regis prodeunt;
Fulget Crucis mysterium,
Qua vita mortem pertulit,
Et morte vitam protulit.

Quæ vulnerata lanceæ
Mucrone diro, criminum
Ut nos lavaret sordibus,
Manavit unda et sanguine.

Impleta sunt quæ concinit
David fideli carmine,
Dicendo nationibus:
Regnavit a ligno Deus.

Arbor decora et fulgida,
Ornata Regis purpura,
Electa digno stipite,
Tam sancta membra tangere.

Beata cujus brachiis
Pretium pependit sæculi,
Statera facta corporis,
Tulitque prædam tartari.

O Crux, ave, spes unica,
Hoc Passionis tempore,
Piis adauge gratiam,
Reisque dele crimina.

Te, fons salutis, Trinitas,
Collaudet omnis spiritus;
Quibus Crucis victoriam
Largiris, adde præmium.   Amen.

HYMN.

Behold the royal ensigns fly,
Bearing the Cross's mystery;
Where life itself did death endure,
And by that death did life procure.

A cruel spear let out a flood
Of water mixed with saving blood;
Which, gushing from our Saviour's side,
Drowned our offences in the tide.

The mystery we now unfold
Which David's faithful verse foretold,
Of our Lord's kingdom, whilst we see
God ruling nations from a tree.

A lovely tree, whose branches bore
The royal purple of His gore;
How glorious does Thy body shine,
Supporting members so divine!

The world's blest balance Thou wast made,
Thy happy beams its purchase weighed,
And bore His limbs who snatched away
Devouring hell's expecting prey.

Hail Cross, our hope! to thee we call,
Who keep this mournful festival,
Grant to the just increase of grace,
And every sinner's crimes efface.

Blest Trinity, we praises sing,
To Thee from whom all graces spring;
Celestial crowns on those bestow
Who conquer by the cross below.   Amen.

RESOLUTION.

O Lord Jesus, after having contemplated
Thy features disfigured by sorrow, meditated on
Thy Passion with compunction, can our hearts
but be filled with love for Thee and hatred
against sin, which even this day outrages Thy
Adorable Face? Do not permit us, O Lord, to
rest satisfied with a sterile compassion; make us
worthy children of Mary, and grant us, as to
Thy divine Mother, the grace to follow Thee to
Calvary, in order that the opprobriums which
await Thee, O Jesus, may affect us more, and

STABAT MATER.

Stabat Mater dolorosa,
Juxta crucem lacrymosa,
Dum pendebat filius.

Cujus animam gementem,
Contristatem et dolentem,
Pertransivit gladius.

O quam tristis et afflicta,
Fuit illa benedicta
Mater unigeniti!

Quæ merebat et dolebat,
Et tremebat, cum videbat
Nati pœnas incliti.

make us also enter courageously on the way of expiation and of true love. Amen.

Sweet Heart of Jesus, be my refuge!

O my merciful Jesus!

May the holy names of Jesus, Mary, and Joseph, be known, blessed, and glorified in all places. Amen.

We thank Thee, O Lord, for all Thy benefits, and we beseech Thee to sink deep in our hearts the sentiments of love and gratitude; place on our lips canticles of praise and thanksgiving now and for all eternity. Amen.

STABAT MATER.

Beneath the world's redeeming wood,
The most afflicted Mother stood,
Mingling her tears with her Son's Blood.

As that flowed down from every part,
Of all His wounds she felt the smart,
What pierced His body pierced her heart.

Who can with tearless eyes look on,
When such a Mother, such a Son,
Wounded and gasping does bemoan!

O worse than Jewish heart, that could
Unmoved behold the double flood
Of Mary's tears and Jesu's Blood.

Quis est homo, qui non fleret,
Christi matrem si videret,
In tanto supplicio?

Quis posset non contristari
Piam matrem contemplari
Dolentem cum filio?

Pro peccatis suæ gentis
Vidit Jesum in tormentis,
Et flagellis subditum.

Vidit suum dulcem natum
Morientem, desolatum,
Dum emisit spiritum.

Eja, mater fons amoris,
Me sentire vim doloris
Fac ut tecum lugeam.

Fac ut ardeat cor meum,
In amando Christum Deum,
Ut sibi complaceam.

Sancta mater istud agas,
Crucifixi fige plagas
Cordi meo valide.

Tui nati vulnerati,
Jam dignati pro me pati
Pœnas mecum divide.

Alas, our sins, they were not His,
In this atoning sacrifice,
For which He bleeds, for which He dies.

When graves were opened, rocks were rent,
When nature and each element,
His torments and her grief resent:

Shall man, the cause of all His pain,
And all His grief, shall sinful man,
Alone insensible remain?

Ah, pious Mother, teach my heart,
Of sighs and tears the only art,
And in thy grief to bear a part.

The sword of grief which did pass through,
Thy very soul, O may it now
Upon my heart a wound bestow.

Great Queen of Sorrows, in thy train
Let me a mourner's place obtain,
With tears to cleanse all sinful stain.

To heal the leprosy of sin
We must the cure with tears begin,
All flesh 's corrupt without their brine.

Refuge of sinners, grant that we
May tread thy steps, and let it be
Our sorrow not to grieve like thee.

Fac me vere tecum flere,
Crucifixo condolere,
Donec ego vixero.

Juxta crucem tecum stare
Te libenter sociare,
In planctu desiderio.

Virgo virginum præclara,
Mihi jam non sis amara
Fac me tecum plangere.

Fac ut portem Christi mortem,
Passionis fac consortem,
Et plagas recolere.

Fac me plagis vulnerari
Cruce hac inebriari
Ob amorem filii.

Inflamatus et accensus,
Per te virgo sim defensus,
In die judicii.

Fac me cruce custodiri,
Morte Christi præmuniri
Confoveri gratia.

Quando corpus morietur,
Fac ut animæ donetur
Paradisi gloria. Amen.

O may the wounds of thy dear Son
Our contrite hearts possess alone,
And all terrene affections drown.

Those wounds which now the stars outshine,
Those furnaces of love divine,
May they our drossy souls refine,

And on us such impressions make,
That we of suffering for His sake,
May joyfully our portion take.

Let us His proper badge put on,
Let's glory in the cross alone,
By which He marks us for His own.

That when the dreadful trial's come,
For every man to hear his doom,
On His right hand we may find room.

O hear us, Mary! Jesus, hear!
Our humble prayers secure our fear,
When Thou in judgment shalt appear.

Now give us sorrow, give us love,
That so prepared we may remove,
When called to seats in bliss above.   Amen.

TEXTS FROM HOLY SCRIPTURE,

RELATIVE TO THE HOLY FACE OF OUR SAVIOUR
WHICH MAY SERVE FOR INSTRUCTION, OR A
PRAYERS TO HONOUR THE HOLY FACE.

" For this was I born, and for this came I into the world
that I should give testimony to the truth : every one that is
of the truth heareth my voice."— John xviii. 27.

GOSPEL.

" At that time the high-priest said to Him, I
adjure Thee by the Living God, that Thou tell
us if Thou be the Christ, the Son of the Living.
Jesus saith to them: Thou hast said it. Nevertheless, I say to you, hereafter you shall see the
Son of Man sitting on the right hand of the

power of God, and coming in the clouds of heaven. Then the high priest rent his garments, saying: He hath blasphemed: what further need have we of witnesses? Behold now you have heard the blasphemy? What think you? But they answering, said: He is guilty of death. Then did they spit in His Face, and buffet Him, and others struck His Face with the palms of their hands, saying: Prophesy unto us, O Christ, who is it that struck Thee?—*St. Matt.* xxvi. 63-67.

DISPOSITIONS.

Seek ye the Lord and His power: seek ye His Face evermore.—I. *Paral.* xvi. 11.

Give alms out of thy substance, and turn not away thy face from any poor person; for so it shall come to pass that the Face of the Lord shall not be turned from Thee.—*Tobias* iv. 7.

Be not hasty to depart from His Face, and do not continue in an evil work; for He will do all that pleaseth Him.—*Ecclesiastes* viii. 3.

Turn to the Lord and forsake thy sins. Make thy prayer before the face of the Lord, and offend less.—*Ecclesiasticus* xvii. 21-22.

PRAYERS.

The Lord shew His Face to thee, and have mercy on thee. The Lord turn His countenance to thee, and give thee peace.—*Num.* vi. 25-26.

Arise, O Lord, and let Thine enemies be scattered, and let them that hate Thee flee from before Thy face.—*Num.* x. 35.

O Lord God, turn not away the Face of Thy anointed : remember the mercies of David Thy servant.—II. *Paral.* vi. 42.

The light of Thy Countenance, O Lord, is signed upon us ; Thou hast given gladness in my heart.—*Ps.* iv. 7.

How long, O Lord, wilt Thou forget me unto the end ? how long dost Thou turn away Thy Face from me.—*Ps.* xii. 2.

But as for me, I will appear before Thy sight in justice; I shall be satisfied when Thy glory shall appear.—*Ps.* xvi. 15.

In Thy sight, O Lord, the king shall rejoice ; and in Thy salvation he shall rejoice exceedingly. Thou hast given him his heart's desire, and hast not withholden from him the will of his lips. For Thou shalt give Him to be a blessing for ever and ever, Thou shalt make him joyful in gladness with Thy countenance.—*Ps.* xx. 1, 2, 7.

Who shall ascend into the mountain of the Lord, or who shall stand in His holy place? The innocent in hands, and the clean of heart, who hath not taken his soul in vain, nor sworn deceitfully to his neighbour. He shall receive a blessing from the Lord, and mercy from God his Saviour. This is the generation of them that seek Him, of them that shall seek the face of the God of Jacob.—*Ps.* xxiii. 3-6.

My heart hath said to thee: My Face hath sought thee; Thy Face, O Lord, will I still seek. Turn not away Thy Face from me; decline not in Thy wrath from Thy servant.—*Ps.* xxvi. 8, 9.

Make Thy Face to shine: save me in Thy mercy.—*Ps.* xxx. 17.

The eyes of the Lord are upon the just, and His ears unto their prayers. But the countenance of the Lord is against them that do evil things, to cut off the remembrance of them from the earth.—*Ps.* xxxiii. 16-17.

Why turnest Thou Thy Face away, and forgettest our want and our trouble?—*Ps.* xliii. 24.

Turn away Thy Face from my sins, and blot out all mine iniquities. Create a clean heart in me, O God; and renew a right spirit within my bowels. Cast me not away from Thy Face, and take not Thy Holy Spirit from me.—*Ps.* l. 11, 12, 13.

May God have mercy on us, and bless us. May He cause the light of His Countenance to shine upon us, and may He have mercy on us. That we may know Thy way upon earth, Thy

salvation upon all nations. Let people confess to
Thee, O God; let all people give praise to Thee.
Let the nations be glad and rejoice; for Thou
judgest the peoples with justice, directest the
nations upon earth.—*Ps.* lxvi. 2—5.

Hear me, O Lord, for Thy mercy is kind;
look upon me, according to the multitude of Thy
tender mercies. And turn not away Thy Face
from Thy servant, for I am in trouble: hear
me speedily.—*Ps.* lxviii. 17, 18.

O God of Hosts, convert us, and shew Thy
Face, and we shall be saved.—*Ps.* lxxix. 8.

Turn again, O God of Hosts, look down from
heaven, and see, and visit this vineyard. Things
set on fire and dug down shall perish at the
rebuke of Thy countenance. Let Thy hand be
upon the man of Thy right hand, and upon the
Son of Man whom Thou hast confirmed upon
Thyself. And we depart not from Thee, Thou
shalt quicken us, and we will call upon Thy
name.—*Ps.* lxxix. 15, 17, 18, 19.

O Lord God of Hosts convert us, and shew
Thy Face and we shall be saved.—*Ps.* lxxix. 20.

Behold, O God, our protector, and look on the
Face of Thy Christ.—*Ps.* lxxxiii. 10.

Lord, why castest Thou off my prayer? why
turnest Thou away Thy Face from me?—*Ps.*
lxxxvii. 15.

Justice and judgment are the preparation of
Thy throne; mercy and truth shall go before

Thy Face. Blessed is the people that knoweth jubilation, they shall walk, O Lord, in the light of Thy countenance.—*Ps.* lxxxviii. 15, 16.

Hear, O Lord, my prayer; and let my cry come to Thee. Turn not away Thy Face from me: in the day when I am in trouble, incline Thy ear to my prayer.—*Ps.* ci. 2-3.

I entreated Thy Face with all my heart: have mercy on me, according to Thy word. Make Thy Face to shine upon Thy servant, and teach me Thy justifications.—*Ps.* cxviii. 58 and 135.

O Lord God, turn not away the Face of Thy anointed: remember the mercies of David Thy servant.—!I. *Paral.* vi. 42.

For Thy servant David's sake, turn not away the Face of Thy anointed. For the Lord hath chosen Sion; He hath chosen it for His dwelling. This is My rest for ever and ever: here will I dwell, for I have chosen it. There will I bring forth a horn to David; I have prepared a lamp for My anointed.—*Ps.* cxxxi. 10, 13, 14, and 17.

Hear me speedily, O Lord: my spirit hath fainted away. Turn not away Thy Face from me, lest I be like unto them that go down into the pit.—*Ps.* cxliii. 7.

THANKSGIVING.

Ye that fear the Lord, praise Him: all ye the seed of Jacob, glorify Him. Let all the seed of Israel fear Him ; because He hath not slighted nor despised the supplication of the poor man ; neither hath He turned away His Face from me ; and when I cried to Him He heard me.— *Ps.* xxi. 24-5.

Come let us praise the Lord with joy ; let us joyfully sing to God our Saviour. Let us come before His presence with thanksgiving, and make a joyful noise to Him with psalms. For the Lord is a great God, and a great King above all gods.—*Ps.* xciv. 1, 2, 3.

Seek ye the Lord and be strengthened: seek His Face evermore.—*Ps.* civ. 4.

AN ACT OF PRAISE.

May the most holy, most sacred, most ador-able name of God, be praised, blessed, loved, adored, and glorified in heaven, on earth, and in hell, by all the creatures of God, and by the Sacred Heart of our Lord and Saviour Jesus Christ in the Most Holy Sacrament of the Altar. Amen.

MY JESUS, SAY, WHAT WRETCH HAS DARED?

My Jesus, say, what wretch has dared
 Thy sacred hands to bind?
And who has dared to buffet so
 Thy face so meek and kind?
  'Tis I have thus ungrateful been,
   Yet, Jesus, pity take:
  O spare and pardon me, my Lord,
   For Thy sweet mercy's sake.

My Jesus, who with spittle vile
 Profaned Thy sacred brow?
And whose unpitying scourge has made
 Thy precious Blood to flow?

My Jesus, whose the hands that wove
 That cruel thorny crown?
Who made that hard and heavy cross
 Which weighs Thy shoulders down?

My Jesus, who has mocked Thy thirst
 With vinegar and gall?
Who held the nails that pierced Thy hands,
 And made the hammer fall?

My Jesus, say, who dar'd to nail
 Those tender feet of Thine?
And whose the arm that raised the lance
 To pierce that heart divine? Amen.

LITANY OF THE HOLY FACE,

IN REPARATION FOR BLASPHEMIES,

AND TO IMPLORE OF GOD, BY THE ADORABLE FACE OF HIS SON, ANY GRACE, AND ESPECIALLY THE CONVERSION OF SINNERS.

Lord, have mercy on us.

Christ, have mercy on us.

Lord, have mercy on us.

Christ, hear us.

Christ, graciously hear us.

Holy Mary, pray for us.

O Adorable Face, which wast adored with profound respect by Mary and Joseph when they saw Thee for the first time. Have mercy on us.

O Adorable Face, which in the stable of Bethlehem didst ravish with joy the angels, the shepherds, and the wise men,

O Adorable Face, which in the Temple didst transpierce with a dart of love holy Simeon and the prophetess Anna,

O Adorable Face, which wast bathed in tears in Thy holy Infancy,

O Adorable Face, which, appearing in the Temple, didst fill with admiration the Doctors of the Law,

O Adorable Face, whose charms were so ravishing, and whose grace was so attrac-

Have mercy on us.

O Adorable Face, whose nobility characterized every feature,

O Adorable Face, contemplated by the Angels,

O Adorable Face, sweet delectation of the Saints,

O Adorable Face, masterpiece of the Holy Ghost, in which the Eternal Father is well pleased,

O Adorable Face, delight of Mary and Joseph,

O Adorable Face, ineffable mirror of the divine perfections,

O Adorable Face, which appeasest the anger of God,

O Adorable Face, which makest the devils tremble,

O Adorable Face, treasure of grace and blessing,

O Adorable Face, exposed in the desert to the inclemencies of the weather,

O Adorable Face, which wast bathed with sweat in Thy journeys, and scorched with the heat of the sun,

O Adorable Face, whose expression was all divine,

O Adorable Face, whose modesty and meekness attracted both just and sinners,

O Adorable Face, troubled and weeping at the tomb of Lazarus,

Have mercy on us.

O Adorable Face, brilliant as the sun, and radiant with glory on Mount Thabor,

O Adorable Face, sorrowful at the sight of Jerusalem, and shedding tears over that ungrateful city,

O Adorable Face, bowed to the earth in the Garden of Olives, and covered with confusion for our sins,

O Adorable Face, bathed in a bloody sweat,

O Adorable Face, kissed by the perfidious Judas,

O Adorable Face, whose sanctity and majesty struck the soldiers with fear, and cast them to the ground,

O Adorable Face, struck by an infamous servant, blindfolded and profaned by the sacrilegious hands of Thy enemies,

O Adorable Face, defiled with spittl, and bruised by so many buffets and blows,

O Adorable Face, whose divine look wounded the heart of Peter with repentant sorrow and love,

O Adorable Face, humbled for us at the tribunals of Jerusalem,

O Adorable Face, which preserved Thy serenity when Pilate pronounced the fatal sentence,

O Adorable Face, covered with sweat and

Have mercy on us.

blood, and falling int the mire under the weight of the cross,

O Adorable Face, wiped with a veil by a pious woman, on the road to Calvary,

O Adorable Face, raised on the instrument of the most shameful punishment,

O Adorable Face, whose incomparable beauty was obscured under the fearful cloud of the sins of the world,

O Adorable Face, covered with the sad shades of death,

O Adorable Face, washed and anointed by Mary and the holy women, and covered with a shroud,

O Adorable Face, enclosed in the sepulchre,

O Adorable Face, all resplendent with glory and beauty on the day of the resurrection,

O Adorable Face, all dazzling with light at the moment of Thy ascension,

O Adorable Face, hid in the Eucharist,

O Adorable Face, which wilt appear at the end of time in the clouds, with great power and majesty,

O Adorable Face, which wilt cause sinners to tremble,

O Adorable Face, which wilt fill the just with joy for all eternity,

Have mercy on us.

Lamb of God, who takest away the sins of the world: *Spare us, O Lord !*

Lamb of God, who takest away the sins of the world: *Graciously hear us, O Lord !*

Lamb of God, who takest away the sins of the world: *Have mercy on us !*

PRAYER.

I salute, adore, and love Thee, O Jesus, my Saviour, covered anew with outrages by blasphemers, and I offer Thee, through the heart of Thy blessed Mother, the worship of all the Angels and Saints, as an incense and a perfume of sweet odour, most humbly beseeching Thee, by the virtue of Thy Sacred Face, to repair and renew in me and, in all men Thy image disfigured by sin. Amen.

ANOTHER PRAYER.

I salute, adore, and love Thee, O Adorable Face of Jesus, my Beloved, noble Seal of the Divinity; with all the powers of my soul I apply myself to Thee, and pray Thee most humbly to imprint in us all the features of Thy divine likeness. Amen. Pater. Ave. Gloria.

A rescript of our Most Holy Father Pius IX., dated January 27, 1858, grants one hundred days indulgence which may be applied to the souls in Purgatory, each time that any one recites the above Litany and prayers, adding to each verse of the Litany, " Gloria Patri," &c.

Printed by Richardson and Son, Derby.

www.ingramcontent.com/pod-product-compliance
Lightning Source LLC
Chambersburg PA
CBHW020303090426
42735CB00009B/1196